Class Sche

Time	Monday	Tuesday	Wednesday	Thursday	Friday	Saturday	Sunday

Made in the USA
Middletown, DE
07 October 2020

21366791R00057